Shadowed Secrets

Shadowed Secrets

Matthew Petchinsky

Shadowed Secrets: Groundhog Day Mysteries
By: Matthew Petchinsky

Introduction: Exploring the Mystery of Groundhog Day and Its Origins

Groundhog Day, celebrated annually on February 2nd, is a curious and endearing tradition that bridges folklore, superstition, and the natural cycles of the seasons. Rooted in ancient practices and modernized in its current whimsical form, the holiday revolves around a humble creature—the groundhog—emerging from its burrow to predict the weather. While it may seem like a lighthearted observance today, the origins of Groundhog Day are steeped in deep cultural significance and an enduring connection to humanity's desire to understand and harmonize with the rhythms of nature.

Ancient Roots: Tying Weather to Spirituality

The origins of Groundhog Day trace back thousands of years to ancient pagan and agrarian societies. These communities closely monitored seasonal changes, as their survival depended on planting and harvesting at the right times. February 2nd falls at a pivotal juncture in the calendar year, marking the midpoint between the winter solstice and the spring equinox. For many cultures, this period symbolized a time of transition—a heralding of brighter days and the eventual arrival of spring.

One of the most notable predecessors to Groundhog Day is the Celtic festival of Imbolc. Celebrated in honor of Brigid, the goddess of fertility, poetry, and renewal, Imbolc was a time for rituals that invoked blessings on the land and sought signs of spring's arrival. These traditions involved observing animals, particularly burrowing creatures like badgers or hedgehogs, to divine whether the harshness of winter would soon fade. Over time, these practices migrated and adapted as they merged with other cultural influences.

Christian Integration: Candlemas Day

With the spread of Christianity across Europe, many pagan traditions were incorporated into Christian observances. February 2nd became known as Candlemas Day, commemorating the presentation of Jesus at the temple. On this day, clergy blessed candles that symbolized light and hope for the remaining winter months. Similar to earlier pagan customs, Candlemas carried weather-related superstitions. Folklore held that clear and sunny weather on Candlemas Day indicated a longer, harsher winter, while cloudy or stormy conditions signaled the arrival of an early spring.

This intersection of faith and folklore set the stage for Groundhog Day as we know it. As European immigrants brought these beliefs to North America, they adapted their practices to the local wildlife. The groundhog, a native creature familiar to settlers, replaced the hedgehog as the weather-predicting animal of choice.

The Groundhog Takes Center Stage

The modern celebration of Groundhog Day began in the 18th and 19th centuries with German-speaking immigrants who settled in Pennsylvania. Drawing on their traditions of weather divination, they imbued the groundhog with an almost mystical significance. The tradition gained widespread popularity in Punxsutawney, Pennsylvania, where it became an annual event in 1887. Today, Punxsutawney Phil, the famous groundhog, emerges from his burrow in Gobbler's Knob each year to deliver his much-anticipated weather forecast.

Though the accuracy of Phil's predictions is often debated, the spectacle and symbolism of the event remain a beloved cultural phenomenon. Groundhog Day serves as a playful reminder of humanity's age-old fascination with nature's cycles and our desire to glimpse the future, even if only through the shadow of a small woodland creature.

The Deeper Meaning Behind the Ritual

At its heart, Groundhog Day is more than just a quirky celebration. It is a reflection of humanity's enduring hope and resilience during the long, dark days of winter. It reminds us of our connection to the natural world and the importance of observing and respecting its patterns. For centuries, people have looked to this time of year for reassurance—a promise that the cold and hardship of winter will eventually yield to warmth and renewal.

In a broader sense, Groundhog Day speaks to the universal human yearning for certainty in an uncertain world. Whether through ancient rituals, weather lore, or modern meteorology, the holiday embodies the timeless quest to find meaning and predictability in the ever-changing tapestry of life.

A Celebration of Whimsy and Heritage

Today, Groundhog Day stands as a unique blend of folklore, history, and community celebration. While its roots lie in the practical needs and spiritual practices of our ancestors, the holiday has evolved into a cherished moment of levity in the depths of winter. Whether it is celebrated with festivals, parades, or simple curiosity, Groundhog Day invites us to pause, reflect, and appreciate the enduring mysteries of nature and tradition.

In this exploration of Groundhog Day's origins and meaning, we delve into its fascinating history, its cultural evolution, and its modern-day significance. As we uncover the layers of this seemingly simple tradition, we discover a rich tapestry of human connection, hope, and timeless wonder.

Chapter 1: The Myth of the Shadow

The legend of the groundhog's shadow is the cornerstone of Groundhog Day, captivating imaginations and sparking conversations each February. While the sighting of a groundhog's shadow may seem like a simple weather prediction today, this myth has deep roots in folklore, cultural symbolism, and humanity's intrinsic connection to nature. The shadow, both literal and metaphorical, holds a profound place in the collective psyche, intertwining superstition, storytelling, and ancient beliefs about the changing seasons.

Shadows in Mythology and Folklore

Shadows have long been imbued with mystical and symbolic meaning in cultures around the world. From ancient myths to philosophical musings, shadows often represent duality—the interplay between light and dark, the known and unknown, life and death. In many traditions, a shadow can be seen as a reflection of the soul or a harbinger of fate.

The myth of the shadow as a weather omen ties directly to this duality. On Groundhog Day, the appearance of the groundhog's shadow signifies the persistence of winter, while its absence heralds the arrival of spring. This dichotomy mirrors humanity's age-old desire to make sense of nature's cycles and find balance between hope and caution.

The Evolution of the Groundhog's Shadow as a Weather Omen

The specific belief that an animal's shadow can predict the weather has its roots in European folklore. German settlers brought the practice of weather divination to North America, where it became intertwined with the traditions of Candlemas Day. In Germany, it was the hedgehog whose shadow served as a weather predictor, rooted in the idea that certain animals could sense seasonal changes more acutely than humans.

When these settlers arrived in Pennsylvania, they replaced the hedgehog with the groundhog, a creature native to North America and already known for its hibernation habits. The groundhog's behavior aligned well with the existing folklore: emerging from its burrow after a long winter nap to check for signs of spring.

The Shadow as a Scientific Phenomenon

While the myth of the shadow is charming, its basis is purely observational. The appearance of a shadow on Groundhog Day depends entirely on weather conditions. A sunny day casts a shadow, while a cloudy day does not. This simple meteorological fact, however, takes on a much larger symbolic meaning when tied to the changing seasons.

In the natural world, midwinter weather can be unpredictable, with bright sunny days often followed by frigid temperatures. The shadow myth may have originated from this phenomenon, where clear skies during winter often coincide with colder conditions due to high-pressure systems.

The Groundhog and the Shadow: A Relationship Beyond Science

In the realm of folklore, the groundhog's shadow represents more than just weather—it symbolizes uncertainty, duality, and the power of observation. The act of watching for the shadow transforms the groundhog from a simple burrowing animal into a revered oracle of seasonal change. The shadow serves as a metaphorical boundary between winter's harsh grip and spring's rejuvenating embrace.

This symbolic relationship elevates Groundhog Day from mere superstition to a ritual of collective hope. Communities gather to witness the groundhog's emergence, eager to interpret the shadow's meaning. Whether the prediction is taken seriously or simply enjoyed as lighthearted fun, the act itself reinforces a sense of unity and shared anticipation.

Shadows in Psychology and Cultural Contexts

Beyond weather lore, the shadow holds psychological and cultural significance. Swiss psychologist Carl Jung famously used the concept of the "shadow self" to describe the unconscious aspects of one's personality that are often hidden or repressed. In this sense, the groundhog's shadow can be viewed as a reflection of humanity's fears and hopes—our longing to escape the cold and move toward growth and renewal.

In broader cultural contexts, shadows often symbolize mystery and transformation. In literature and art, they represent hidden truths, suppressed emotions, or the promise of something just beyond reach. The groundhog's shadow, therefore, can be seen as a playful yet profound metaphor for life's uncertainties and the human desire to forecast and control the future.

Modern Interpretations of the Shadow Myth

Today, the myth of the shadow remains a central part of Groundhog Day festivities, particularly in Punxsutawney, Pennsylvania. The annual event, centered around Punxsutawney Phil, has become a spectacle of tradition, community, and celebration. Phil's shadow is interpreted by handlers, known as the "Inner Circle," who announce whether winter will persist or spring will arrive early.

While the accuracy of the predictions is debated—scientific studies suggest a success rate of around 39%—the charm of the shadow myth lies not in its precision but in its ability to captivate. The ritual taps into a shared sense of wonder and nostalgia, reminding participants of the ancient ties between humanity and the natural world.

The Shadow as a Bridge Between Past and Present

The enduring power of the groundhog's shadow lies in its ability to connect the past with the present. It is a modern ritual rooted in ancient beliefs, reminding us of humanity's enduring relationship with the environment and our quest to understand the cycles of life. The shadow myth, though playful, invites us to pause and consider the mysteries of the natural world, drawing inspiration from the interplay of light and dark.

Conclusion: The Symbolic Power of the Shadow

The myth of the shadow is far more than a quaint tradition; it is a timeless narrative that resonates deeply with the human spirit. By observing the groundhog and its shadow, we participate in a ritual that bridges folklore, science, and cultural symbolism. It reminds us of the beauty in life's uncertainties and the unyielding hope for brighter days ahead. Groundhog Day, with its focus on the shadow, continues to cast a lasting impression on our hearts and minds, celebrating the cyclical dance of the seasons and our place within it.

Chapter 2: Groundhog Legends from Around the World

Though the groundhog may seem uniquely tied to North American traditions, the themes of weather divination, animal behavior, and seasonal forecasting are universal. Across cultures and centuries, legends of creatures that signal seasonal changes or act as omens of nature's rhythms have captivated societies. These stories, while diverse in their origins, share a common thread: the deep human desire to interpret the natural world for survival and understanding.

In this chapter, we explore groundhog legends alongside similar traditions from around the globe, tracing their evolution and the cultural values they embody.

The Groundhog in North America: The Weather Oracle

The modern celebration of Groundhog Day in North America is centered on the groundhog, a rodent from the marmot family known for its burrowing habits and hibernation cycles. Groundhogs, also called woodchucks, became the focal point of a uniquely American tradition brought over by German immigrants.

Punxsutawney Phil is the most famous of these weather-predicting groundhogs. Every February 2nd, in Punxsutawney, Pennsylvania, Phil is ceremonially "consulted" to predict the remaining duration of winter. According to the tradition:

- If Phil sees his shadow, there will be six more weeks of winter.
- If he does not, an early spring is imminent.

While Punxsutawney Phil's notoriety has made him a cultural icon, other towns have adopted their own weather-predicting groundhogs, such as Wiarton Willie in Canada and Buckeye Chuck in Ohio. These traditions demonstrate how folklore evolves to reflect local pride and community identity.

European Roots: The Hedgehog and Badger as Prophets

The origins of North American groundhog lore can be traced back to **German folklore**. In Germany, it was believed that a hedgehog emerging from its burrow on Candlemas Day (February 2nd) could predict the length of winter. The logic was similar to modern Groundhog Day:

- A sunny day (and the resulting shadow) foretold a longer winter.
- A cloudy day indicated an earlier spring.

When German settlers arrived in Pennsylvania, they adapted this tradition to the native groundhog, as hedgehogs were not native to North America. The groundhog's similar behavior made it a natural substitute for the role of weather prophet.

In other parts of Europe, the **badger** played a similar role. In medieval England, farmers observed badgers on February 2nd as part of their weather predictions. The badger's behavior was believed to signal changes in the seasons, reinforcing humanity's dependence on animal behavior for survival.

Japan: The Cicada and Seasonal Awareness

While Japan does not have a tradition directly involving groundhogs, the **cicada** holds a parallel place in Japanese culture as a harbinger of seasonal changes. Cicadas emerge in late spring and early summer, their piercing songs marking the arrival of warmer weather.

Japanese folklore often connects the behavior of animals to natural phenomena. For example:

- If cicadas emerge early, it is believed that summer will be particularly hot.
- Conversely, their late emergence may indicate an unusual seasonal pattern.

This cultural emphasis on observing nature for guidance mirrors the principles behind Groundhog Day.

China: The Myth of the Ox and Seasonal Divination

In ancient **Chinese folklore**, the ox plays a role akin to the groundhog in signaling seasonal transitions. During **Li Chun**, the solar term marking the beginning of spring, a clay ox was traditionally crafted and displayed. Farmers would use the ox as a symbol to divine the strength and timing of the coming agricultural season.

Additionally, Chinese zodiac animals are often tied to specific years and seasons, with each animal associated with unique qualities that influence the year's fortune. These beliefs showcase the universal human tendency to link animal behavior with natural and spiritual insights.

India: The Cobra and Weather Predictions

In **Indian mythology**, snakes, particularly cobras, are revered as divine creatures that influence weather patterns. During **Nag Panchami**, a festival honoring serpents, offerings are made to snakes to ensure good rains and agricultural prosperity.

The cobra's behavior—such as emerging from its burrow during specific times—is sometimes seen as an omen of forthcoming weather. While this tradition is more spiritual than practical, it highlights a similar reliance on animal activity as a predictor of environmental shifts.

Scandinavia: The Bear as the Keeper of Seasons

In **Scandinavian folklore**, the bear plays a significant role in seasonal myths. Hibernating through the harsh winter months, the bear is seen as a symbol of renewal and fertility when it awakens in the spring. Norse legends often depict bears as mystical creatures connected to the cycles of life and nature.

In rural Scandinavian communities, it was believed that the bear's emergence from its den could forecast the timing of spring. Like the groundhog, the bear's behavior was observed to provide insight into seasonal transitions.

The Arctic: Polar Bears and Inuit Weather Lore

Inuit communities in the Arctic observe the behavior of polar bears and other wildlife to understand environmental patterns. Though there is no specific polar bear equivalent to Groundhog Day, Inuit legends often link the actions of animals to seasonal changes. For example:

- The condition of polar bears' coats was seen as an indicator of winter severity.
- The migration patterns of birds and seals also offered clues about upcoming seasonal shifts.

These practices emphasize the importance of wildlife in predicting and surviving extreme weather conditions.

Africa: Frogs as Rainmakers

In many **African cultures**, frogs are closely associated with rainfall and seasonal changes. In some regions, the croaking of frogs is believed to signal the arrival of rain, essential for agriculture and survival.

Specific myths, such as those of the **rain frog**, highlight the animal's mystical connection to weather. Similar to the groundhog's role in predicting seasonal change, frogs in African folklore are seen as intermediaries between humans and nature.

Australia: The Platypus and Unpredictable Seasons

Australia's unique wildlife has inspired numerous legends tied to nature and weather. The **platypus**, with its unusual appearance and elusive behavior, has been regarded as a mystical creature by Aboriginal Australians. Stories often ascribe weather-related powers to animals, such as predicting rainfall or changes in temperature.

While the platypus does not serve as a direct weather predictor like the groundhog, its role in folklore reflects the broader human tendency to seek meaning in animal behavior.

The Universal Significance of Animal Prophecy

The use of animals to predict weather and seasonal changes is a near-universal phenomenon. From the groundhog in North America to the hedgehog in Europe and the cobra in India, these traditions reveal humanity's reliance on observing nature for guidance. While the animals may differ, the underlying principles remain consistent:

1. Animals are seen as closer to nature and, therefore, more attuned to its cycles.
2. The observation of animal behavior provides a tangible, accessible way to interpret otherwise unpredictable environmental patterns.
3. These traditions foster a sense of unity and continuity within communities, connecting people to their environment and shared heritage.

Conclusion: Legends Beyond Borders

Groundhog Day may seem like a uniquely American tradition, but it is part of a much broader tapestry of animal-based weather lore from around the world. These legends remind us of the universality of human curiosity and the enduring bond between people and the natural world. By exploring the myths of animals like hedgehogs, badgers, and even polar bears, we see that Groundhog Day is not just a quirky holiday—it is a celebration of humanity's timeless effort to harmonize with the rhythms of the Earth.

Chapter 3: The Science Behind the Groundhog's Shadow

The tradition of Groundhog Day, with its whimsical focus on the groundhog's shadow as a weather predictor, may seem more rooted in folklore than in science. However, beneath the charm of this annual ritual lies a fascinating intersection of animal biology, meteorology, and human psychology. Understanding the science behind the groundhog's shadow involves exploring hibernation, seasonal weather patterns, and the broader mechanisms that influence both the groundhog's behavior and the climate.

The Groundhog's Shadow: A Meteorological Perspective

At the heart of Groundhog Day's prediction lies a simple meteorological concept: whether or not the groundhog sees its shadow depends entirely on the day's weather conditions. Here's how it works:

- **A sunny day** means clear skies, which allow sunlight to cast a shadow. According to tradition, this indicates six more weeks of winter.
- **An overcast day** prevents the groundhog from casting a shadow, symbolizing an early arrival of spring.

From a scientific perspective, this interpretation is symbolic rather than predictive. The presence of a shadow does not directly correlate with the duration or severity of winter, but the weather on February 2nd is influenced by larger atmospheric patterns that may give clues about seasonal trends.

Hibernation: The Groundhog's Seasonal Cycle

The behavior of groundhogs during winter hibernation plays a critical role in their selection as weather predictors. Groundhogs are true hibernators, meaning they undergo significant physiological changes during the cold months, including:

1. **Lowered Body Temperature:** Groundhogs reduce their body temperature to as low as 38°F (3°C) to conserve energy.
2. **Slowed Metabolism:** Their heart rate drops from about 80 beats per minute to as low as 5 beats per minute, and their breathing slows dramatically.
3. **Energy Conservation:** Groundhogs rely on fat reserves accumulated during the summer and fall to sustain them through the winter.

Hibernation is triggered by environmental cues, such as decreasing daylight hours and falling temperatures, which also align with the seasonal changes that affect weather. Groundhogs typically emerge from hibernation in late winter or early spring to mate, which coincides with the timing of Groundhog Day. Their emergence is not tied to weather prediction but rather to biological and environmental rhythms.

The Role of Photoperiodism

One scientific explanation for the timing of the groundhog's emergence is **photoperiodism**—the physiological response of organisms to changes in day length. As the days grow longer after the winter solstice, groundhogs and other hibernating animals sense the shift and begin preparing to wake from their winter slumber. This process is governed by the release of hormones like melatonin, which regulates sleep cycles and seasonal behaviors.

While this natural timing aligns with the Groundhog Day tradition, it is not influenced by immediate weather conditions. Instead, it reflects the animal's internal biological clock and the gradual shift toward spring.

Weather Patterns and Seasonal Predictions

The science of seasonal weather prediction, known as **phenology**, is far more complex than the Groundhog Day tradition suggests. Meteorologists rely on data from atmospheric and oceanic patterns, such as the **El Niño-Southern Oscillation (ENSO)** and the **polar vortex**, to forecast seasonal trends.

- **El Niño and La Niña:** These oceanic phenomena influence global weather patterns, including the severity of winters and the timing of seasonal changes.
- **The Polar Vortex:** This band of strong winds encircles the Arctic and affects the distribution of cold air across the Northern Hemisphere. A weakened polar vortex can lead to prolonged cold spells, while a stable one keeps cold air confined to the Arctic.

While these phenomena provide valuable insights, their complexity and variability mean that long-term weather predictions remain an inexact science. Groundhog Day's shadow tradition simplifies this intricate process into an accessible and entertaining ritual.

The Psychology of Weather Folklore

One of the reasons the Groundhog Day tradition endures is its psychological appeal. Humans are naturally inclined to seek patterns and meaning in the world around them, and weather has always been a significant factor in survival and comfort.

- **Confirmation Bias:** People are more likely to remember predictions that align with actual weather outcomes, reinforcing the belief in the groundhog's accuracy.
- **The Need for Certainty:** In the unpredictable and often harsh winter months, the tradition offers a sense of control and optimism about the future.
- **Community and Storytelling:** Groundhog Day provides an opportunity for communities to come together and share in a

lighthearted celebration, which strengthens social bonds and cultural continuity.

Groundhog Day Accuracy: Fact or Fiction?

The accuracy of groundhog-based weather predictions has been a subject of much debate and study. Scientific analyses suggest that groundhogs' predictions are correct about **39% of the time**, which is slightly worse than random chance. However, this does not diminish the charm or cultural significance of the tradition.

Meteorologists, who rely on advanced technology and data models, achieve significantly higher accuracy rates in short-term forecasts but face similar challenges in long-term predictions. This highlights the limitations of both folklore and science in forecasting complex weather systems.

The Symbolism of Shadows

From a scientific standpoint, the shadow itself is simply the result of light being blocked by an object. On Groundhog Day, the shadow's appearance depends on the angle and intensity of sunlight, which vary with the time of year and geographic location. However, the shadow holds deeper cultural and psychological meaning.

In literature and mythology, shadows often symbolize uncertainty, fear, or the unknown. In the context of Groundhog Day, the groundhog's shadow serves as a metaphor for the lingering grip of winter and the hope for renewal that comes with spring. This symbolic layer adds depth to an otherwise straightforward weather ritual.

The Climate Change Factor

As climate change alters global weather patterns, the traditional cycles of hibernation and seasonal change are also being affected. Warmer winters may disrupt the groundhog's natural hibernation schedule, causing them to emerge earlier or remain active longer. These shifts could challenge the timing and relevance of Groundhog Day in the future.

Additionally, the variability introduced by climate change makes long-term weather predictions more difficult, even for scientists. This underscores the need to understand and mitigate the impacts of climate change on ecosystems and traditions alike.

Conclusion: Bridging Science and Tradition

The science behind the groundhog's shadow reveals a fascinating blend of biology, meteorology, and human psychology. While the tradition of Groundhog Day may not hold up to scientific scrutiny as a reliable weather prediction method, it serves a greater purpose by connecting people to the natural world and fostering a sense of wonder.

By exploring the interplay between animal behavior, environmental cues, and atmospheric phenomena, we gain a deeper appreciation for both the science and the folklore that shape this enduring tradition. Groundhog Day reminds us that even in the age of advanced meteorology, there is room for mystery, storytelling, and the simple joy of watching a groundhog emerge from its burrow.

Chapter 4: Decoding the Groundhog's Forecast

Groundhog Day centers on a seemingly simple ritual: the groundhog emerges from its burrow, and whether or not it sees its shadow dictates the length of winter. Beneath this straightforward tradition, however, lies a nuanced and layered practice that involves interpreting nature, understanding the groundhog's behavior, and reconciling folklore with modern meteorology. Decoding the groundhog's forecast requires examining the symbolic, scientific, and cultural dimensions of this cherished tradition.

The Ritual: Observing the Groundhog's Behavior

Each year on February 2nd, the groundhog's emergence becomes the focal point of national and international attention. The ritual unfolds in a ceremonial manner, with communities eagerly awaiting the pronouncement of the groundhog's prediction. Key elements of the forecast include:

1. **Shadow Sighted:** If the groundhog sees its shadow, it is believed that winter will persist for six more weeks.
2. **No Shadow:** If the groundhog does not see its shadow, spring is predicted to arrive early.

While the ritual appears straightforward, the process involves an intricate interplay of natural phenomena, human interpretation, and cultural storytelling.

Interpreting the Shadow: A Meteorological Perspective

From a meteorological standpoint, the presence or absence of the groundhog's shadow is determined by local weather conditions on Groundhog Day:

- **Clear Skies:** High-pressure systems often bring clear skies and colder weather, making shadows more likely.
- **Cloudy Skies:** Low-pressure systems typically cause overcast conditions and milder temperatures, reducing the chance of a shadow.

These atmospheric patterns align with broader weather trends, providing some logic to the groundhog's forecast. However, it is important to note that a single day's weather conditions are not a reliable predictor of the remaining winter season. Long-term weather patterns are influenced by global phenomena, such as the jet stream, ocean currents, and polar air masses.

The Role of Human Interpretation

The forecast is delivered not by the groundhog itself but by human intermediaries, often dressed in formal attire and serving as part of the "Inner Circle" in locations like Punxsutawney, Pennsylvania. These individuals interpret the groundhog's behavior, adding a layer of theatricality and communal engagement to the event.

This act of human interpretation introduces subjectivity into the forecast, emphasizing the ritualistic and symbolic nature of Groundhog Day over its scientific accuracy. The interpretation process transforms a natural occurrence into a shared cultural moment, reinforcing the event's social and celebratory significance.

Cultural and Psychological Significance of the Forecast

The groundhog's forecast resonates deeply with the human psyche, tapping into universal themes of hope, renewal, and the desire to understand the future. The symbolic power of the forecast lies in its ability to:

1. **Alleviate Seasonal Anxiety:** For many, the dark and cold days of winter are challenging, both physically and emotionally. Groundhog Day offers a lighthearted way to break up the monotony and look forward to the arrival of spring.
2. **Create a Shared Narrative:** The ritual fosters a sense of community, as people collectively participate in the anticipation and interpretation of the groundhog's prediction.
3. **Celebrate the Cycles of Nature:** By focusing on the groundhog's behavior, the tradition connects participants to the rhythms of the natural world, emphasizing the continuity of seasonal change.

Forecast Accuracy: Myth vs. Reality

The accuracy of the groundhog's forecast has been the subject of debate and scrutiny. Scientific studies suggest that the predictions are correct about 39% of the time, a success rate lower than chance. Despite this, the tradition endures, driven more by its cultural charm than its meteorological precision.

Factors that contribute to the variability in forecast accuracy include:

- **Regional Weather Differences:** A single groundhog's forecast cannot account for the diverse climate patterns across different geographic areas.
- **Global Weather Influences:** Large-scale phenomena like El Niño and La Niña have significant impacts on seasonal weather, which cannot be predicted by observing local conditions on a single day.

Meteorologists use sophisticated tools and models to forecast weather with much higher accuracy, but the simplicity and folklore of the groundhog's method remain appealing.

The Symbolism of the Shadow and Seasonal Change

The groundhog's shadow carries rich symbolic meaning, representing more than just the presence or absence of sunlight. In folklore and mythology, shadows often symbolize:

- **Uncertainty and Fear:** The shadow can evoke the lingering grip of winter and the challenges associated with it.
- **Hope and Renewal:** The absence of a shadow signals the promise of spring and the renewal of life.

This dual symbolism reflects humanity's relationship with the natural world, where cycles of hardship and growth are intertwined. The shadow becomes a metaphor for the unpredictable nature of life and the resilience required to navigate it.

Modern Adaptations and Regional Variations

While Punxsutawney Phil is the most famous groundhog, other regions have adopted their own versions of the tradition, each with unique adaptations and interpretations:

- **Wiarton Willie (Canada):** This albino groundhog from Ontario delivers Canada's version of the forecast, adding an international dimension to the tradition.
- **Staten Island Chuck (New York):** Known for his bold personality, Chuck is a popular figure in New York City's Groundhog Day celebrations.
- **Buckeye Chuck (Ohio):** Ohio's official weather predictor adds local flavor to the nationwide ritual.

These regional variations highlight the adaptability of the tradition, allowing communities to make it their own while preserving its core essence.

The Groundhog's Forecast in a Changing Climate

As climate change alters weather patterns and seasonal cycles, the relevance and accuracy of the groundhog's forecast face new challenges. Warmer winters and shifting ecological behaviors may impact the groundhog's hibernation cycle, potentially disrupting the timing of its emergence.

Furthermore, the unpredictability introduced by climate change makes long-term seasonal forecasting more complex, emphasizing the importance of understanding and mitigating its effects on both ecosystems and cultural traditions.

Conclusion: The Charm of Decoding the Forecast

Decoding the groundhog's forecast reveals a tradition that is as much about storytelling and community as it is about nature and weather. While the scientific accuracy of the groundhog's prediction may be limited, its cultural and symbolic significance cannot be overstated. The ritual invites us to engage with the rhythms of the natural world, celebrate the approach of spring, and find joy in the shared experience of interpreting the shadow.

Ultimately, the groundhog's forecast is less about precise meteorology and more about the timeless human desire to connect with the mysteries of nature and the hope that each new season brings. By embracing both the science and the folklore of Groundhog Day, we honor the enduring magic of this beloved tradition.

Chapter 5: Mystical Interpretations of Groundhog Day

While Groundhog Day is widely celebrated as a quirky weather-predicting tradition, its mystical undertones are often overlooked. Beneath the lighthearted surface lies a rich tapestry of spiritual symbolism, astrological connections, and metaphysical ideas that resonate deeply with humanity's collective consciousness. Groundhog Day, with its focus on shadows, cycles, and nature, invites mystical interpretations that reveal layers of meaning far beyond its folklore origins.

The Shadow as a Spiritual Symbol

Shadows are potent symbols in spiritual and mystical traditions worldwide. Often representing the unseen, the unconscious, or hidden truths, the shadow embodies duality—the balance between light and darkness, known and unknown, seen and unseen. In the context of Groundhog Day, the groundhog's shadow can be interpreted as a metaphor for:

1. **Inner Reflection:** The shadow invites us to confront aspects of ourselves that we may suppress or ignore, much like Carl Jung's concept of the "shadow self."
2. **Transformation and Renewal:** Seeing the shadow signals the lingering presence of winter, a period of introspection and dormancy, while its absence heralds spring's energy of growth and renewal.
3. **The Cyclical Nature of Life:** The interplay between light and shadow reflects the eternal cycle of death and rebirth, echoing the rhythms of nature.

This dual symbolism makes Groundhog Day a spiritual metaphor for balancing inner darkness and light to embrace personal growth and renewal.

Astrological Connections to Groundhog Day

Groundhog Day falls on February 2nd, a date that holds significant astrological importance. It occurs during the zodiac sign of Aquarius, known for its forward-thinking, innovative, and humanitarian qualities. Mystically, Aquarius represents:

- **The Air Element:** A time for ideas, inspiration, and insight, aligning with the hope of an early spring.
- **Transition and Change:** Aquarius energy bridges the gap between winter's introspection and spring's rebirth, much like Groundhog Day itself.

Additionally, February 2nd is situated near the midpoint of the seasonal calendar between the winter solstice and the spring equinox, marking a period of balance and anticipation. This time, known as a **cross-quarter day**, has been celebrated in various spiritual traditions, including:

- **Imbolc (Celtic):** A festival honoring Brigid, the goddess of fertility, renewal, and inspiration, symbolizing the first stirrings of spring.
- **Candlemas (Christian):** A day associated with purification and the return of light, reinforcing themes of spiritual renewal and hope.

Astrologically and spiritually, Groundhog Day aligns with these transitional energies, making it a potent moment for reflection, intention-setting, and honoring nature's cycles.

Mythical Archetypes in Groundhog Day

The groundhog itself can be seen as a mythical archetype, embodying themes and qualities that resonate with mystical traditions. Some interpretations include:

1. **The Guardian of the Threshold:** The groundhog's emergence from its burrow symbolizes crossing a threshold between two worlds—winter and spring, darkness and light, introspection and action. Mystically, this can be interpreted as a rite of passage or initiation into a new phase.
2. **The Seer or Oracle:** The groundhog's ability to "predict" the weather places it in the role of a divine messenger or prophet, bridging the earthly and celestial realms.
3. **The Hermit:** During hibernation, the groundhog embodies the archetype of the hermit, retreating into solitude for rest and renewal. Its emergence mirrors the mystical journey of returning to the world with newfound wisdom.

These archetypes give Groundhog Day a deeper resonance, linking it to universal spiritual themes of transformation and insight.

The Elemental Mysticism of Groundhog Day

Groundhog Day's connection to the natural world evokes the power of the four classical elements—Earth, Air, Fire, and Water—which are central to many mystical traditions:

1. **Earth:** The groundhog, a burrowing creature, is deeply tied to the Earth element, symbolizing stability, introspection, and the cycles of life.
2. **Air:** The atmospheric conditions on Groundhog Day—clear skies or overcast clouds—invoke the Air element, representing change, perception, and clarity.
3. **Fire:** The sun, whose presence determines the shadow, embodies the Fire element, signifying illumination, energy, and transformation.
4. **Water:** The melting snow and the promise of spring's rains reflect the Water element, symbolizing renewal, fertility, and emotional healing.

Together, these elements create a mystical framework for interpreting Groundhog Day as a celebration of nature's interconnectedness and the harmony of elemental forces.

Groundhog Day and the Lunar Cycle

Though the tradition does not explicitly reference the moon, the mystical significance of shadows ties Groundhog Day to lunar symbolism:

- **The Shadow of the Moon:** In mystical practices, the moon's shadow represents mystery, intuition, and the subconscious, themes that align with the spiritual meaning of the groundhog's shadow.
- **Seasonal Alignment:** February often coincides with the waxing or full moon, a time associated with manifestation, heightened awareness, and preparation for growth.

By linking Groundhog Day to lunar cycles, we can interpret the ritual as a reflection of the moon's influence on nature, emotions, and spiritual transformation.

Groundhog Day as a Portal of Transformation

In mystical traditions, liminal spaces—moments between two states of being—are considered powerful opportunities for change and spiritual awakening. Groundhog Day, situated between the solstice and equinox, serves as a portal for:

- **Letting Go:** Releasing the stagnation of winter, both physically and emotionally.
- **Setting Intentions:** Planting the seeds of goals and aspirations for the coming spring.
- **Renewing Connection:** Deepening one's relationship with nature and the cycles of the Earth.

By viewing Groundhog Day as a mystical portal, individuals can harness its energy for personal growth, ritual practices, and spiritual alignment.

Rituals and Mystical Practices for Groundhog Day

For those seeking to infuse Groundhog Day with mystical significance, consider the following rituals and practices:

1. **Shadow Work Journaling:** Reflect on aspects of yourself that you've avoided or hidden, using the shadow as a metaphor for personal growth.
2. **Seasonal Intention Setting:** Meditate on your goals for the coming spring and write them down, focusing on renewal and transformation.
3. **Nature Observation:** Spend time in nature, observing the subtle signs of seasonal change, and honor the Earth's cycles with gratitude.
4. **Candle Lighting:** Light candles to symbolize the return of light and clarity, aligning with the themes of Candlemas and Imbolc.

These practices can deepen your connection to the mystical aspects of Groundhog Day, transforming it into a meaningful spiritual observance.

The Collective Energy of Groundhog Day

Groundhog Day's widespread celebration creates a collective energy that transcends individual experiences. This shared focus amplifies the mystical potential of the day, as millions of people direct their attention to themes of hope, renewal, and seasonal change. In mystical terms, this collective consciousness can:

- **Manifest Positive Change:** The shared energy of anticipation and celebration can create a ripple effect, fostering optimism and unity.
- **Strengthen Spiritual Connection:** By participating in a global ritual, individuals tap into the collective wisdom and energy of humanity's relationship with nature.

This collective dimension elevates Groundhog Day from a localized tradition to a universal expression of hope and renewal.

Conclusion: Embracing the Mystical Essence of Groundhog Day

Groundhog Day, though often viewed as a lighthearted tradition, is steeped in mystical significance. Its focus on shadows, cycles, and nature invites us to explore deeper spiritual truths about balance, transformation, and the rhythms of life. By embracing the mystical interpretations of Groundhog Day, we can honor its rich symbolism and use it as a tool for personal and collective growth.

Whether through reflection, ritual, or community celebration, Groundhog Day offers a unique opportunity to connect with the mystical forces that shape our world and our lives. It reminds us that even the simplest traditions can hold profound meaning, bridging the earthly and the spiritual in a timeless dance of light and shadow.

Appendix A: Historical Facts and Fun Trivia About Groundhog Day

Groundhog Day is one of the most enduring and beloved traditions in North America, blending folklore, meteorology, and cultural celebration. Its history is filled with fascinating facts, quirky trivia, and amusing anecdotes that enrich the holiday's charm. This appendix explores the historical evolution of Groundhog Day, its iconic traditions, and lesser-known tidbits that reveal the depth and whimsy of this unique celebration.

Historical Facts About Groundhog Day

1. **Origins in Candlemas and Imbolc**
   - Groundhog Day traces its roots to **Candlemas**, a Christian holiday celebrated on February 2nd, marking the midpoint between the winter solstice and spring equinox. In medieval Europe, Candlemas was associated with weather lore, such as:
     - "If Candlemas Day be fair and bright, winter will have another flight."
   - The tradition also aligns with **Imbolc**, a Celtic festival honoring Brigid, the goddess of fertility and renewal, where animal behavior was observed to divine seasonal changes.

2. **The German Hedgehog Tradition**
   - German immigrants to Pennsylvania brought the tradition of using animals for weather prediction. In Germany, the **hedgehog** was the chosen creature, believed to have mystical abilities to sense weather shifts. Upon settling in North America, they replaced the hedgehog with the native **groundhog**.

3. **The First Groundhog Day Celebration**
    ◦ The first official Groundhog Day was celebrated on February 2, 1887, in **Punxsutawney, Pennsylvania**. The event was organized by local newspaper editor Clymer Freas, who declared Punxsutawney the "Weather Capital of the World" and made **Punxsutawney Phil** the centerpiece of the tradition.

4. **Punxsutawney Phil's Inner Circle**
    ◦ The **Inner Circle**, a group of tuxedo-clad individuals, manages Punxsutawney Phil's appearances and predictions. This secretive group adds an air of ceremony and humor to the tradition, interpreting Phil's "forecast" in "Groundhogese."

5. **Phil's Official Record**
    ◦ Punxsutawney Phil's predictions are meticulously recorded in the **Groundhog Day records**, which track his shadow sightings since the 1800s. However, his forecasting accuracy is often debated, with scientific studies showing a success rate of about **39%**.

6. **Canada's Wiarton Willie**
    ◦ Canada has its own famous groundhog: **Wiarton Willie** from Ontario. The albino groundhog's predictions have been celebrated since 1956, making him a northern counterpart to Punxsutawney Phil.

7. **Other Notable Groundhogs**
    ◦ Across North America, various regions have their own weather-predicting groundhogs, including:
        ▪ **Staten Island Chuck** in New York
        ▪ **General Beauregard Lee** in Georgia
        ▪ **Buckeye Chuck** in Ohio
        ▪ **Balzac Billy** in Alberta, Canada

Fun Trivia About Groundhog Day

1. **The Name "Woodchuck"**
   - The groundhog is also known as a **woodchuck**, deriving its name from the Algonquian word **"wuchak."** Despite the tongue twister, groundhogs have nothing to do with chucking wood!

2. **Phil's Long Life**
   - According to folklore, Punxsutawney Phil is over **135 years old**, thanks to an "elixir of life" he drinks every summer. In reality, groundhogs typically live **6-8 years** in the wild.

3. **The Shadow Rule**
   - Groundhog Day's rules state that a **shadow means six more weeks of winter**, while **no shadow means an early spring**. However, this simplistic method is more tradition than meteorology.

4. **Groundhog Day in Pop Culture**
   - The 1993 film **"Groundhog Day"**, starring Bill Murray, brought international attention to the holiday. The movie's concept of reliving the same day repeatedly has become a cultural metaphor for monotony and second chances.

5. **Phil's Full Name**
   - Punxsutawney Phil's official name is **"Punxsutawney Phil, Seer of Seers, Sage of Sages, Prognosticator of Prognosticators, and Weather Prophet Extraordinary."**

6. **The Groundhog's Burrow**
   - Groundhogs are expert diggers, creating extensive burrow systems that can be **20-30 feet long** with multiple cham-

bers. These burrows serve as their homes during hibernation and are crucial to their survival.

7. **The Largest Groundhog Day Event**
   - Punxsutawney's celebration at Gobbler's Knob attracts over **20,000 visitors** annually, making it the largest Groundhog Day event in the world. Festivities include music, fireworks, and live entertainment.

8. **Phil's Media Appearances**
   - Punxsutawney Phil has made appearances on major TV networks, including **The Oprah Winfrey Show** and **The Today Show**, cementing his status as a cultural icon.

Groundhog Day Superstitions

1. **Good Luck for the Year**
   - Some believe that attending a Groundhog Day event brings good luck and prosperity for the rest of the year, especially if the groundhog predicts an early spring.

2. **The Significance of Clear Skies**
   - In folklore, sunny skies on February 2nd were considered an omen of extended hardship (winter), while cloudy skies symbolized hope and renewal.

3. **Phil's Meteorological Powers**
   - According to legend, Punxsutawney Phil is the only true weather-predicting groundhog, and all others are mere imitators.

Groundhog Biology: Fun Facts

1. True Hibernators
   - Groundhogs are true hibernators, lowering their heart rate to **5 beats per minute** and their body temperature to **38°F (3°C)** during the winter months.

2. Diet and Appetite
   - Groundhogs are herbivores and can consume over **1 pound of vegetation** daily during summer to build fat reserves for hibernation.

3. Burrow Engineers
   - Groundhogs' burrows have multiple entrances and chambers, including a designated "bathroom," demonstrating their engineering prowess.

Groundhog Day's Global Influence

1. German and European Traditions
   - Similar to Groundhog Day, European traditions used animals like hedgehogs or badgers to predict weather. These customs date back centuries and reflect humanity's enduring reliance on nature for guidance.

2. Japanese Groundhog Day?
   - While Japan doesn't celebrate Groundhog Day, festivals like **Setsubun**, marking the transition from winter to spring, share the theme of seasonal renewal.

Conclusion: Groundhog Day's Enduring Legacy

Groundhog Day is more than just a lighthearted tradition; it's a reflection of history, culture, and the human connection to nature's rhythms. From its ancient roots in European folklore to its modern-day celebrations, the holiday has evolved into a cherished event that blends science, superstition, and community. By understanding its historical facts and fun trivia, we gain a deeper appreciation for the charm and significance of this unique celebration.

Whether you're watching Punxsutawney Phil's prediction, exploring the behavior of these fascinating creatures, or simply enjoying the festivities, Groundhog Day offers a delightful opportunity to celebrate the quirks and wonders of the natural world.

<u>Message from the Author:</u>

I hope you enjoyed this book, I love astrology and knew there was not a book such as this out on the shelf. I love metaphysical items as well. Please check out my other books:

-Life of Government Benefits

-My life of Hell

-My life with Hydrocephalus

-Red Sky

-World Domination:Woman's rule

-World Domination:Woman's Rule 2: The War

-Life and Banishment of Apophis: book 1

-The Kidney Friendly Diet

-The Ultimate Hemp Cookbook

-Creating a Dispensary(legally)

-Cleanliness throughout life: the importance of showering from childhood to adulthood.

-Strong Roots: The Risks of Overcoddling children

-Hemp Horoscopes: Cosmic Insights and Earthly Healing

- Celestial Hemp Navigating the Zodiac: Through the Green Cosmos

-Astrological Hemp: Aligning The Stars with Earth's Ancient Herb

-The Astrological Guide to Hemp: Stars, Signs, and Sacred Leaves

-Green Growth: Innovative Marketing Strategies for your Hemp Products and Dispensary

-Cosmic Cannabis

-Astrological Munchies

-Henry The Hemp

-Zodiacal Roots: The Astrological Soul Of Hemp

- **Green Constellations: Intersection of Hemp and Zodiac**

-Hemp in The Houses: An astrological Adventure Through The Cannabis Galaxy

-Galactic Ganja Guide

Heavenly Hemp

Zodiac Leaves

Doctor Who Astrology

Cannastrology

Stellar Satvias and Cosmic Indicas

<u>Celestial Cannabis: A Zodiac Journey</u>

AstroHerbology: The Sky and The Soil: Volume 1

AstroHerbology:Celestial Cannabis:Volume 2

Cosmic Cannabis Cultivation

The Starry Guide to Herbal Harmony: Volume 1

The Starry Guide to Herbal Harmony: Cannabis Universe: Volume 2

Yugioh Astrology: Astrological Guide to Deck, Duels and more

Nightmare Mansion: Echoes of The Abyss

Nightmare Mansion 2: Legacy of Shadows

Nightmare Mansion 3: Shadows of the Forgotten

Nightmare Mansion 4: Echoes of the Damned

The Life and Banishment of Apophis: Book 2

Nightmare Mansion: Halls of Despair

<u>Healing with Herb: Cannabis and Hydrocephalus</u>

<u>Planetary Pot: Aligning with Astrological Herbs: Volume 1</u>

Fast Track to Freedom: 30 Days to Financial Independence Using AI, Assets, and Agile Hustles

<u>Cosmic Hemp Pathways</u>

How to Become Financially Free in 30 Days: 10,000 Paths to Prosperity

Zodiacal Herbage: Astrological Insights: Volume 1

Nightmare Mansion: Whispers in the Walls
The Daleks Invade Atlantis
Henry the hemp and Hydrocephalus

10X The Kidney Friendly Diet
Cannabis Universe: Adult coloring book
Hemp Astrology: The Healing Power of the Stars
Zodiacal Herbage: Astrological Insights: Cannabis Universe: Volume 2
<u>Planetary Pot: Aligning with Astrological Herbs: Cannabis Universes: Volume 2</u>
Doctor Who Meets the Replicators and SG-1: The Ultimate Battle for Survival
Nightmare Mansion: Curse of the Blood Moon
<u>The Celestial Stoner: A Guide to the Zodiac</u>
Cosmic Pleasures: Sex Toy Astrology for Every Sign
Hydrocephalus Astrology: Navigating the Stars and Healing Waters
Lapis and the Mischievous Chocolate Bar

Celestial Positions: Sexual Astrology for Every Sign
Apophis's Shadow Work Journal: : A Journey of Self-Discovery and Healing
Kinky Cosmos: Sexual Kink Astrology for Every Sign
Digital Cosmos: The Astrological Digimon Compendium
Stellar Seeds: The Cosmic Guide to Growing with Astrology
Apophis's Daily Gratitude Journal

Cat Astrology: Feline Mysteries of the Cosmos
The Cosmic Kama Sutra: An Astrological Guide to Sexual Positions
Unleash Your Potential: A Guided Journal Powered by AI Insights
Whispers of the Enchanted Grove

Cosmic Pleasures: An Astrological Guide to Sexual Kinks

369, 12 Manifestation Journal

Whisper of the nocturne journal(blank journal for writing or drawing)

The Boogey Book

Locked In Reflection: A Chastity Journey Through Locktober

Generating Wealth Quickly:

How to Generate $100,000 in 24 Hours

Star Magic: Harness the Power of the Universe

The Flatulence Chronicles: A Fart Journal for Self-Discovery

The Doctor and The Death Moth

Seize the Day: A Personal Seizure Tracking Journal

The Ultimate Boogeyman Safari: A Journey into the Boogie World and Beyond

Whispers of Samhain: 1,000 Spells of Love, Luck, and Lunar Magic: Samhain Spell Book

Apophis's guides:

Witch's Spellbook Crafting Guide for Halloween

<u>Frost & Flame: The Enchanted Yule Grimoire of 1000 Winter Spells</u>

<u>The Ultimate Boogey Goo Guide & Spooky Activities for Halloween Fun</u>

Harmony of the Scales: A Libra's Spellcraft for Balance and Beauty

The Enchanted Advent: 36 Days of Christmas Wonders

Nightmare Mansion: The Labyrinth of Screams

Harvest of Enchantment: 1,000 Spells of Gratitude, Love, and Fortune for Thanksgiving

The Boogey Chronicles: A Journal of Nightly Encounters and Shadowy Secrets

The 12 Days of Financial Freedom: A Step-by-Step Christmas Countdown to Transform Your Finances

Sigil of the Eternal Spiral Blank Journal

A Christmas Feast: Timeless Recipes for Every Meal

Holiday Stress-Free Solutions: A Survival Guide to Thriving During the Festive Season

Yu-Gi-Oh! Holiday Gifting Mastery: The Ultimate Guide for Fans and Newcomers Alike

Holiday Harmony: A Hydrocephalus Survival Guide for the Festive Season

Celestial Craft: The Witch's Almanac for 2025 – A Cosmic Guide to Manifestations, Moons, and Mystical Events

Doctor Who: The Toymaker's Winter Wonderland

Tulsa King Unveiled: A Thrilling Guide to Stallone's Mafia Masterpiece

Pendulum Craft: A Complete Guide to Crafting and Using Personalized Divination Tools

Nightmare Mansion: Santa's Eternal Eve

Starlight Noel: A Cosmic Journey through Christmas Mysteries

The Dark Architect: Unlocking the Blueprint of Existence

Surviving the Embrace: The Ultimate Guide to Encounters with The Hugging Molly

The Enchanted Codex: Secrets of the Craft for Witches, Wiccans, and Pagans

Harvest of Gratitude: A Complete Thanksgiving Guide

Yuletide Essentials: A Complete Guide to an Authentic and Magical Christmas

Celestial Smokes: A Cosmic Guide to Cigars and Astrology

Living in Balance: A Comprehensive Survival Guide to Thriving with Diabetes Insipidus

Cosmic Symbiosis: The Venom Zodiac Chronicles

The Cursed Paw of Ambition

Cosmic Symbiosis: The Astrological Venom Journal

Celestial Wonders Unfold: A Stargazer's Guide to the Cosmos (2024-2029)

The Ultimate Black Friday Prepper's Guide: Mastering Shopping Strategies and Savings

Cosmic Sales: The Astrological Guide to Black Friday Shopping

Legends of the Corn Mother and Other Harvest Myths

Whispers of the Harvest: The Corn Mother's Journal

The Evergreen Spellbook

The Doctor Meets the Boogeyman

The White Witch of Rose Hall's SpellBook

The Gingerbread Golem's Shadow: A Study in Sweet Darkness

The Gingerbread Golem Codex: An Academic Exploration of Sweet Myths

The Gingerbread Golem Grimoire: Sweet Magicks and Spells for the Festive Witch

The Curse of the Gingerbread Golem

10-minute Christmas Crafts for kids

<u>Christmas Crisis Solutions: The Ultimate Last-Minute Survival Guide</u>

Gingerbread Golem Recipes: Holiday Treats with a Magical Twist

The Infinite Key: Unlocking Mystical Secrets of the Ages

Enchanted Yule: A Wiccan and Pagan Guide to a Magical and Memorable Season

Dinosaurs of Power: Unlocking Ancient Magick

Astro-Dinos: The Cosmic Guide to Prehistoric Wisdom

Gallifrey's Yule Logs: A Festive Doctor Who Cookbook

The Dino Grimoire: Secrets of Prehistoric Magick

The Gift They Never Knew They Needed

The Gingerbread Golem's Culinary Alchemy: Enchanting Recipes for a Sweetly Dark Feast

A Time Lord Christmas: Holiday Adventures with the Doctor

Krampusproofing Your Home: Defensive Strategies for Yule

Silent Frights: A Collection of Christmas Creepypastas to Chill Your Bones

Santa Raptor's Jolly Carnage: A Dino-Claus Christmas Tale

Prehistoric Palettes: A Dino Wicca Coloring Journey

The Christmas Wishkeeper Chronicles

The Starlight Sleigh: A Holiday Journey

Elf Secrets: The True Magic of the North Pole

Candy Cane Conjurations

Cooking with Kids: Recipes Under 20 Minutes

Doctor Who: The TARDIS Confiscation

The Anxiety First Aid Kit: Quick Tools to Calm Your Mind

Frosty Whispers: A Winter's Tale

The Infinite Key: Unlocking the Secrets to Prosperity, Resilience, and Purpose

The Grasping Void: Why You'll Regret This Purchase

Astrology for Busy Bees: Star Signs Simplified

The Instant Focus Formula: Cut Through the Noise

The Secret Language of Colors: Unlocking the Emotional Codes

Sacred Fossil Chronicles: Blank Journal

The Christmas Cottage Miracle

Feeding Frenzy: Graboid-Inspired Recipes

Manifest in Minutes: The Quick Law of Attraction Guide

The Symbiote Chronicles: Doctor Who's Venomous Journey

Think Tiny, Grow Big: The Minimalist Mindset

The Energy Key: Unlocking Limitless Motivation

New Year, New Magic: Manifesting Your Best Year Yet

Unstoppable You: Mastering Confidence in Minutes

Infinite Energy: The Secret to Never Feeling Drained

Lightning Focus: Mastering the Art of Productivity in a Distracted World

Saturnalia Manifestation Magick: A Guide to Unlocking Abundance During the Solstice

Graboids and Garland: The Ultimate Tremors-Themed Christmas Guide

12 Nights of Holiday Magic

The Power of Pause: 60-Second Mindfulness Practices

If you want solar for your home go here: https://www.harborso-lar.live/apophisenterprises/

Get Some Tarot cards: https://www.makeplayingcards.com/sell/apophis-occult-shop

<u>Get some shirts: https://www.bonfire.com/store/apophis-shirt-emporium/</u>

<u>**Instagrams:**</u>
@apophis_enterprises,
@apophisbookemporium,
@apophisscardshop
Twitter: @apophisenterpr1
 Tiktok:@apophisenterprise
Youtube: @sg1fan23477, @FiresideRetreatKingdom
Hive: @sg1fan23477
CheeLee: @SG1fan23477

Podcast: Apophis Chat Zone: https://open.spotify.com/show/5zXbrCLEV2xzCp8ybrfHsk?si=fb4d4fdbdce44dec

Newsletter: https://apophiss-newsletter-27c897.beehiiv.com/

If you want to support me or see posts of other projects that I have come over to: **<u>buymeacoffee.com/mpetchinskg</u>**
I post there daily several times a day

Get your Dinowicca or Christmas themed digital products, especially Santa Raptor songs and other musics. Here: **https://sg1fan23477.gumroad.com**

Apophis Yuletide Digital has not only digital Christmas items, but it will have all things with Dinowicca as well as other Digital products.